Index

Purses, Totes, Beach Fun - pages 4 - 5

Jewelry, Purse, Shoes - pages 6 - 8

Layers Bag, Round Purse - page 8

Wine Holder and Yoke Purse - page 9

Bag and Scarf - page 10

Koozie & Woven Bag - page 27

Scarves pages 28 - 29

Jacket and Yoke Purse pages 30 - 31

Baby Bibs - pages 32 - 33

Baby & Children - pages 32 - 33

Easy Dresses - pages 34 - 35

More Tips -
For appliques, I usually secure fusible web to the back of fabrics before I die cut the shapes. Or you can cut first, then fuse.

It is easy to 'fussy cut' pieces after you die cut the master shape. This is good for bodies and to make layers.

Cut a 'snowflake' of butterflies or shapes, by folding a square twice to make a smaller square. Place both folds just 'inside' the cut lines so they stay together when cut.

Wearables on the GO! 3

Sand Dollars at the Beach

Animal Print Rag Bag
Feeling wild tonight? Animal prints are so hot..hot...hot. Get in on the action without the posh price. This rag bag is both easy and inexpensive to make.
instructions on page 12

Shell Scarf
Sparkling beaches update a sand colored scarf. Antique silk shimmers with new life when crystal beads and pearls wash up against yo-yo sand dollars and eyelash yarn seaweed.
instructions on pages 12 - 13

Sea Shell Tank Top
Whether you are on the beach or simply wish you were, this shell and bead bedecked tank top is a summer wardrobe must-have.
instructions on page 13

Sea Shell Beach Bag
Surfs up! Sand dollar yo-yos and seashell beads turn an everyday rattan carry-all into your favorite beach bag.
instructions on page 13

Wearables on the GO! 5

Sunny Citrus

Yo-Yo Flowers Purse
Express your talent and creativity with layered yo-yo flowers. Bamboo handles make this purse comfortable to carry.

instructions on page 14

Fabric Bracelet
Create your own fashion with a stretchy bangle in fabrics to match your favorite outfit.

instructions on page 14

Citrus Fun Shoes
I'm walkin' on sunshine! You'll feel great and step out in style. Brighten your day with fun footwear.

instructions on page 14

Wearables on the GO!

Jewelry on the GO!

From Trash to Treasures Jewelry

"My favorite art pieces develop from used and recycled objects. These are made from water bottle caps, sewing machine bobbins and empty thread spools. I hope these necklaces and bracelets inspire you to think outside the bead box."

instructions on pages 15 - 16

Wearables on the GO! 7

Rag Bag Purse

Got scraps? This roomy Rag Bag is just right for toting your stuff all over town. Sporting 17 different prints, this one-of-a-kind purse stands out in a crowd.

instructions on page 11

Scrap Scarf

Don't throw away that pile of threads and tiny clippings! Turn them into a stunning haute couture accessory with this fast and fabulous technique.

instructions on page 11

Rag Bag

photo is on page 10

SIZE: 10" x 20"

YARDAGE: I used *Studio e fabrics* "SoHo" by BJ Lantz

Prints: 6 yds x 45" all prints combined
The bag requires 53 two-sided rag squares. Use as many different prints as you desire. I used all 17 variations of the "SoHo" fabric.
Solid color woven cotton: 2¾ yds x 45 each of 3 complimentary solid colors
Sewing machine, needle
5 spools of contrasting thread (Kelly Green)
AccuQuilt® GO!™ Fabric Cutter (#55100)
GO! Die Rag Square 5¼" (#55033)

ASSEMBLY:
1. **Handles:** Cut 10 strips 3" x 30" strips (4 print and 2 each of the solids).
2. **Bag:** Cut remaining solid and print fabrics into 12" x 45" strips.
3. Lay fabric on a flat surface. In stacks beginning at bottom, place 1 print face down, place 3 different solids on stack, place final print fabric on top with face up creating 5 layers of fabric.
4. Cut each strip into 6" x 12" strips. Sandwich the straps the same way.
5. **Fabric Stacks:** Using contrasting thread, quilt each stack of 6" x 12" fabric with free motion sewing. Do the same with the strap stacks.

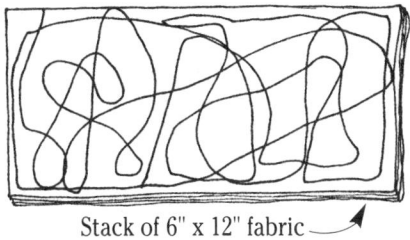

Stack of 6" x 12" fabric

6. **Cutting Parts of Bag:** Use the GO! Fabric Cutter with the Rag Square die and cut 53 squares. Using scissors, carefully cut away the corner squares. Note: Keep cut away squares for Scrap Scarf project.

Remove the corner squares

7. Sew 2 of the squares together with 2 seams. Sew the first seam 1" in from outer edge of fringe and the second seam ¾" from outer edge of fringe. Note: Fringed side is the outside of the bag.

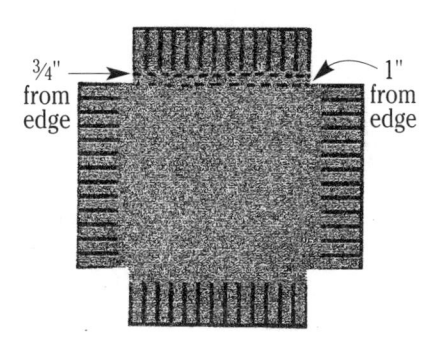

¾" from edge — 1" from edge

8. Join all of the squares into the pattern shown in diagram by first sewing strips and joining the strips together. Pin edges and then sew all edges together.

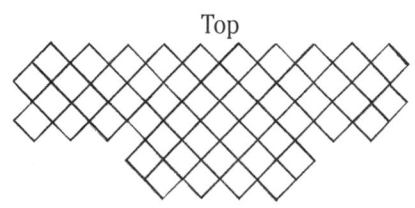

Top

9. Shape bag into a tube, with the fringes on the outside. See diagram for fold lines of bag. Sew the squares together. The squares should fold up and fit together like a puzzle, forming the bottom of the bag. Pin edges and then sew all edges together.

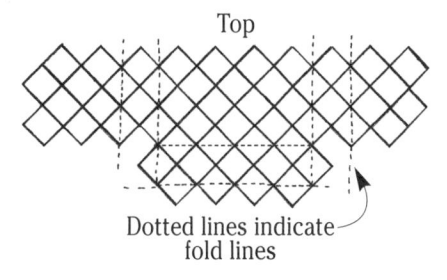

Top

Dotted lines indicate fold lines

10. **Handles:** Fold 3" x 30" sandwich of handle strips into a 1½" x 30" strap. Sew a seam down the open side ¾" from outside edge and a second seam ½" from outer edge.
11. Sew handles to inside of bag on each side. Do not sew on the top half of the top square.

Sew handles to bag

12. **Finish:** Fold top half of all of the squares to the outside and stitch down along fringe. Spritz bag with water and put it in the dryer. This will cause the fringe to bloom.

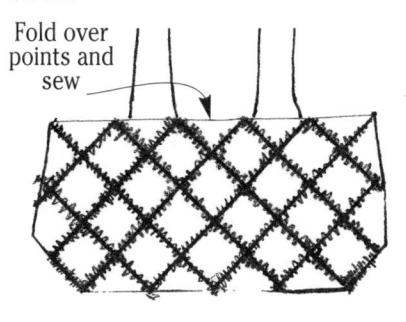

Fold over points and sew

Scrap Scarf

photo is on page 10

SIZE: 6" x 60"

YARDAGE:
Scraps: 1" x 1" corner squares removed from rag square purse
Sulky 100% rayon 40wt thread (Green, Purple, Yellow)
2 pieces of 8" x 60" *Sulky* Ultra Solvy water soluble stabilizer
Yarn, floss, lace, decorative threads
Spray bottle with water
Sewing machine, needle, thread

ASSEMBLY:
Making the scarf: Place Solvy sheet (clear wash away film) on a flat surface. Scatter half of the 1" fabric squares evenly over the Solvy. Drizzle yarn, floss, threads and lace over squares. Scatter remaining squares on top.
Spritz very lightly with water. Lay second Solvy sheet on top and press gently with dry hands. Let dry thoroughly.
Add a few pins to secure. Begin sewing using decorative stitches to connect everything. If desired, couch more yarns on top.

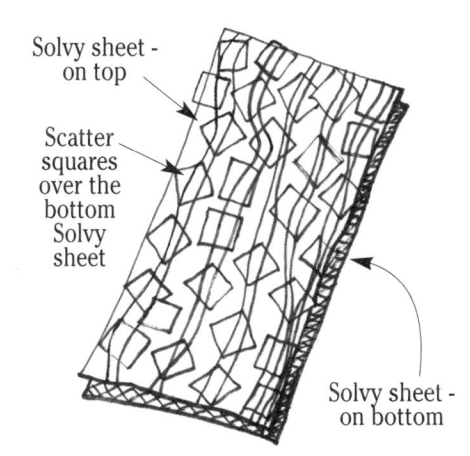

Solvy sheet - on top

Scatter squares over the bottom Solvy sheet

Solvy sheet - on bottom

Remove Solvy: Patti Lee of Sulky of America gave me the best advice about removing Ultra Solvy. Fill your washing machine with water- no clothes or soap. Drop your scarf in and agitate 5-10 minutes. When Solvy is dissolved, remove scarf. Add clothes and laundry soap. The dissolved Solvy will not affect your clothes in any way. Lay the scarf flat to dry.

Wearables on the GO! 11

Animal Print Rag Bag

photo is on page 4

SIZE: 14" x 18"

YARDAGE:
Print 1: ½ yd x 54"
Print 2: ½ yd x 54"
Print 3: 1 yd x 54"
Sewing machine, needle, thread
4 Silver 1½" rings
4 Silver 1¾" pendants
AccuQuilt® GO!™ Fabric Cutter (#55100)
   GO! Die Rag Square 8½" (#55013)

ASSEMBLY:
1. Fold fabric right sides out.
2. With contrasting thread in sewing machine, sew the two layers together with free motion sewing.
3. Cut a section of this fabric 10" x 18" and, using the 8" Rag Square die, cut 2 rag squares.
4. Cut 4 rag squares of color #1, 4 rag squares of color #2, and 5 rag squares of color #3.
5. Also cut two handles 4" x 24" and four tabs 4" x 5½".
6. See Fabric Placement Guide for placement of squares.

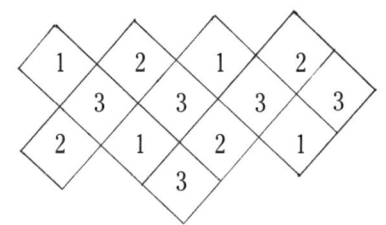

Fabric Placement Guide

7. Sew squares together with the rag edges on the outside, using a 1" seam. Sew again with a ⅞" seam.
8. Close the back by fitting the squares together like a puzzle. Then close the bottom by folding it up toward the back and fitting those squares together.

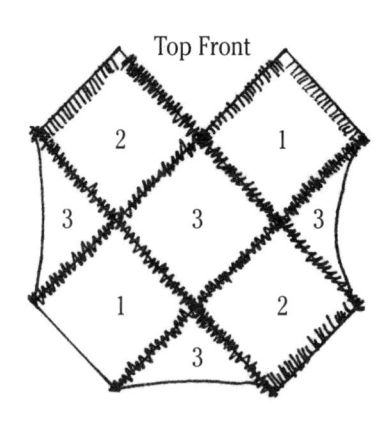

Top Front

9. Fold tabs and handles so that the raw edges are on the center of one side. Turn under raw edges on one side.

10. Overlap the other raw edge. Topstitch closed.

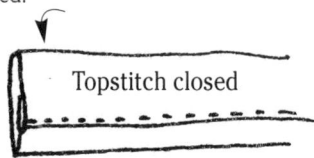

Topstitch closed

11. Topstitch tabs & handles several times in a free motion design.

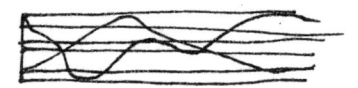

12. At this point, put purse in dryer for 15 minutes to fluff fringes.
13. Put each tab through a ring and even up the ends. Sew the ends of the tabs together.
14. Pin the tabs on the inside of the bag, with 1" of the ringed tab showing above the halfway mark of the square. Attach all 4 tabs.

Inside of bag

15. Cut a rounded corner square, using the same fabrics where the tabs are attached.
16. Turn under the raw edges and hand sew over tab bottoms to form a 'patch'.

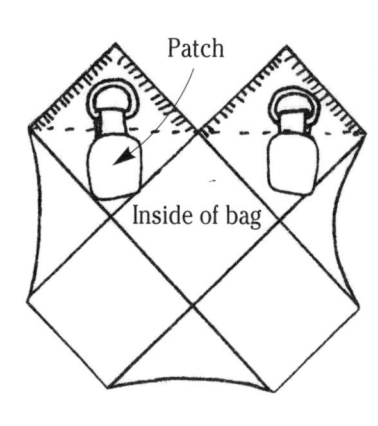

Patch

Inside of bag

17. Fold the points, above the rings, to the outside and machine stitch to purse. Hand-sew a Silver medallion under tabs.

Medallions

18. Push handles through rings, with raw ends on inside of handle. Fold up 2" and sew to handle.
19. Cut 4 handle covers (same tab as handle) 3" x 4½". Turn under tops and bottoms, wrap over raw edges on handles.
20. Turn in raw edges at back and sew seam and top and bottom to handle.

Handle
Covers raw edge

Sea Shell Beach Bag

photo is on page 5

SIZE: 12" x 13"

YARDAGE:
1/3 yd unbleached cotton muslin
Purchased bag
DMC #5 pearl cotton color #437 Off-White
DMC 6 ply embroidery floss #844 Charcoal
5 small shell beads
Embroidery needles for each size thread
AccuQuilt® GO!™ Fabric Cutter (#55100)
   GO! Die Circles – 2", 3", 5" (#55012)

ASSEMBLY:
1. Die cut the following circles: ten 2", eighteen 3", nine 5". Make yo-yos.
2. **Sand Dollars:** Make 4 following the Sand Dollar instructions for Sea Shell Scarf
3. **Sea shell yo-yos:** Using pearl cotton, stitch a spiral of Chain stitches radiating from the center on the gathered side of the yo-yo. Sew a sea shell bead to the center. See Stitch Guide on pages 24 - 25.

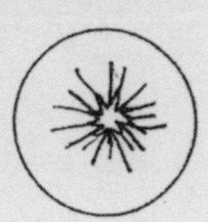

Sea Shell Scarf

photo is on page 5

SIZE: 7" x 58"

YARDAGE:
15 1/4" x 60" Tan silk fabric for scarf
1/3 yd assorted Off-White cotton prints
DMC #5 Gold pearl cotton
DMC 6 ply embroidery floss
   #844 Charcoal
3 1/2 yds Ivory eyelash yarn
Assorted sizes of pearl beads
38 Swarovski Crystal AB 4mm bicone
Mother of Pearl flat beads
Embroidery needles for each size thread
Sewing machine, needle, thread
AccuQuilt® GO!™ Fabric Cutter (#55100)
   GO! Die Circles – 2", 3", 5" (#55012)

ASSEMBLY:
1. **Yo-yos:** From Off-White prints, die cut circles: five 5", four 3", and eight 2". Using the 2" & 3" circles, make yo-yo's. These yo-yo's will use the gathered side as the front.
2. **Sand Dollars:** Make 5 using 5" circles. Use the flat side of the yo-yo. Refer to the Sand Dollar diagram. Using 6 strands of Charcoal floss in a large eye needle, stitch 5 Straight stitches. Come up from the bottom at A and go back down at B. Knot on the back. Add 5 pearl cotton Lazy Daisy stitches and a French Knot in the center. Knot on the back.
See Stitch Guide on pages 24 - 25.

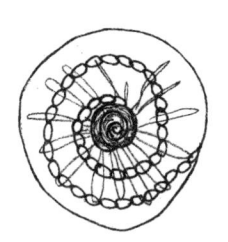

Sea Shell Tank Top

photo is on page 5

YARDAGE:
1/4 yd unbleached cotton muslin
9 small shell beads,
12 Swarovski 4mm crystal AB bicone
40 seed beads (Clear, Silver, Pearl)
DMC #5 pearl cotton color #437 Off-White
DMC 6 ply embroidery floss #844 Charcoal
AccuQuilt® GO!™ Fabric Cutter (#55100)
   GO! Die Circle Cutter 2", 3", 5" (#55012)

ASSEMBLY:
1. Cut the following circles: One 5", Seven 3", Four 2" and make yo-yos.
2. **Sand Dollar:** Make 1 following instructions for Sea Shell Scarf.
3. Using photo on page 5 and diagram below for placement, hand sew all yo-yos, shells and beads in place.

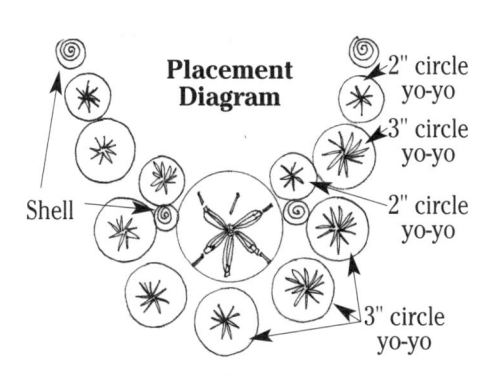

Placement Diagram

Shell
2" circle yo-yo
3" circle yo-yo
2" circle yo-yo
3" circle yo-yo

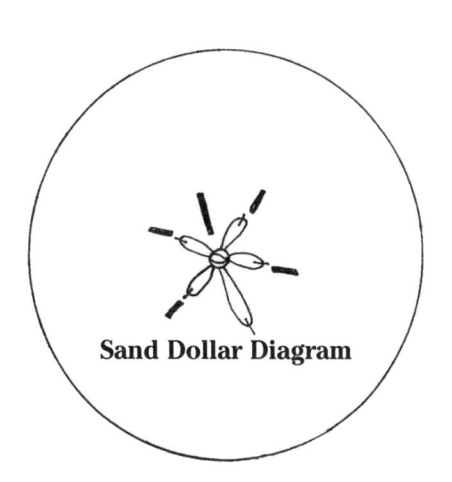

Sand Dollar Diagram

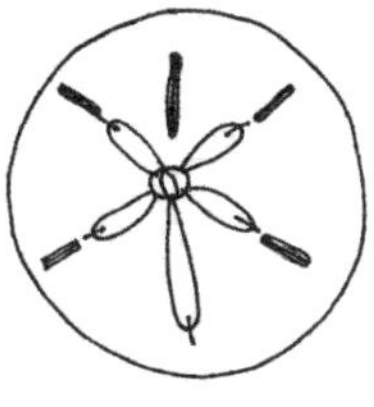

Finished Sand Dollar

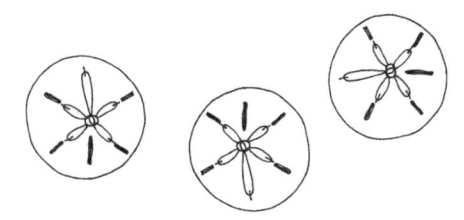

Making a Yo-Yo

GENERAL INSTRUCTIONS:
1. Read through all instructions before beginning.
2. Cut all fabric into circles using the AccuQuilt® GO!™ Fabric Cutter GO!™ Die #55012.
3. Using a needle and a double thread, push the needle in from the wrong side, 1/4" from the outer edge.
4. Fold edge over 1/4", hiding the knot. Sew a Running stitch all the way around the circle, close to the fold. Pull thread, forming a yo-yo.
5. Place a penny, washer, curtain ring or stuffing inside the yo-yo as directed by the individual project and pull the gathering thread tight. Knot securely.

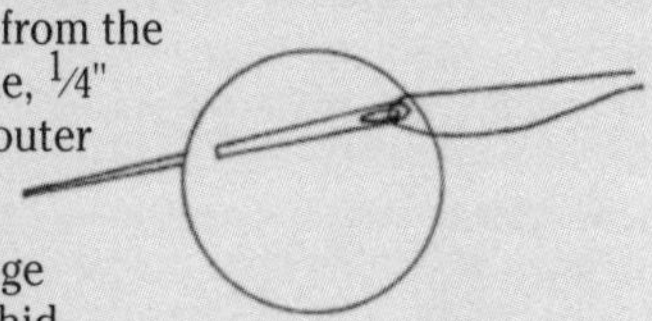

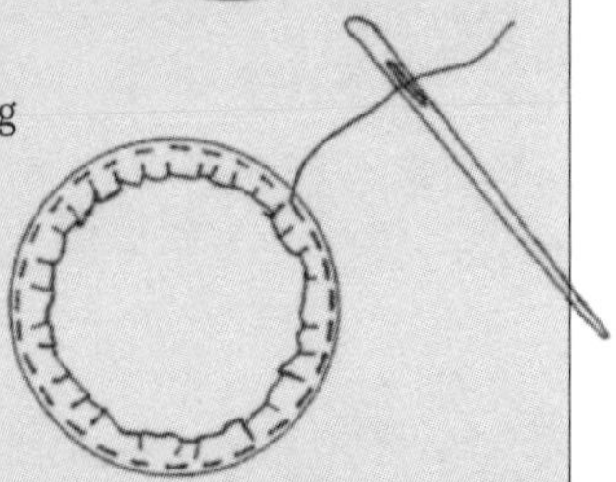

Use Gold pearl cotton for Lazy Daisy stitches and French Knot.
3. **Scarf:** Fold scarf in half lengthwise with the right sides together. Baste together with a 5/8" seam. Press scarf with seam open. Be sure to press side edges.

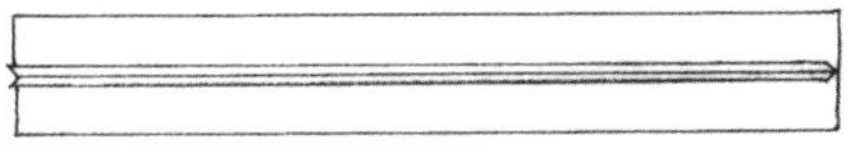

4. Pull out basting thread and use the pressed lines as guide lines for scarf designs.
5. Using a Zigzag stitch, sew the eyelash yarn to the right side of the scarf in a random wavy pattern.
6. Hand sew sand dollars, yo-yo's, pearls, crystals and shell beads to both ends of the scarf on the right side of the fabric, between the pressed lines, leaving 5/8" at the bottom of each scarf end free of decoration.
7. **Finish:** With right sides together, re-sew the back seam and each end. Leave a 3" portion of the center back seam open for turning. Clip corners, turn to right side and close opening with hidden stitches. Press carefully.

Wearables on the GO! 13

Flower Purse

photo is on page 6

SIZE: 14" x 16"

YARDAGE:
I used Clothworks "Folk Dance" by Christine Graf
  3/4 yd x 45" Red print
  Scraps of 8 or 9 coordinating prints
2 yds x 23" Fusible woven 100% cotton stabilizer
6" x 6" sewable fusible web
Two 7" bamboo handles
6 ply Green embroidery floss
Buttons
Sewing machine, needle, thread
AccuQuilt® GO!™ Fabric Cutter (#55100)
  GO! Die 2", 3", 5" circles (#55112)

ASSEMBLY:
1. **Bag:** Back Red print with stabilizer.
2. Using pattern, cut 4 purse sides (2 bags, 2 linings). See diagram for help in cutting bag and lining.

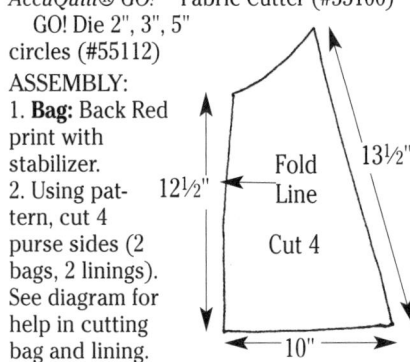

Purse Pattern Diagram

3. Cut 16 handle tabs 2 1/2" x 4". With right sides together, sew 2 purse tab pieces down long sides. Turn to right side, press and topstitch sides 1/4" from edge. Make 8.
4. Cut the following circles: two 5", four Green 3", thirty assorted 3", and two 2". Make yo-yos. See instructions on page 13.
5. **Flowers:** Refer to the Flower diagrams below. Back fabric for two 3" applique circles with fusible web and cut out. Chain stitch 3 stems (Stitch Guide on pages 24-25).

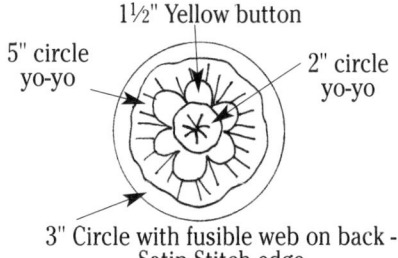

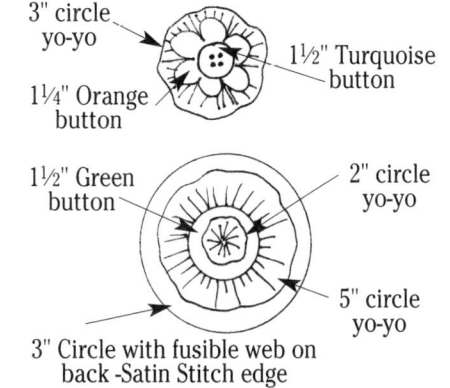

- 5" circle yo-yo
- 1 1/2" Yellow button
- 2" circle yo-yo
- 3" Circle with fusible web on back - Satin Stitch edge

- 3" circle yo-yo
- 1 1/4" Orange button
- 1 1/2" Turquoise button

- 1 1/2" Green button
- 2" circle yo-yo
- 5" circle yo-yo
- 3" Circle with fusible web on back - Satin Stitch edge

6. Position 9 yo-yos on each side and 11 across the bottom of the front of bag, gathered side down, and stitch in place.

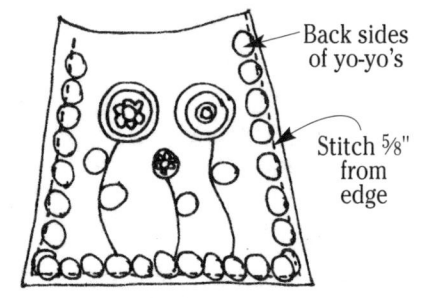

- Back sides of yo-yo's
- Stitch 5/8" from edge

7. **Bag Assembly:** Place back and front of bag right sides together and sew sides and bottom with a 5/8" seam. Stop sewing top sides at dot on each side of the pattern. Repeat for 2 lining pieces.

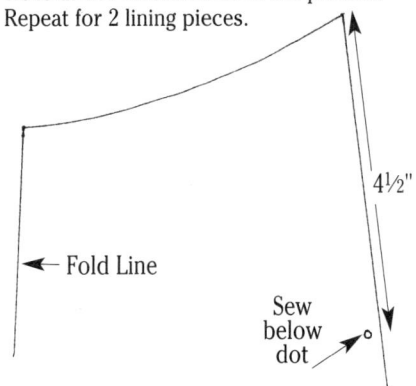

Purse Pattern Diagram

- Fold Line
- Sew below dot
- 4 1/2"

8. Fold 4 tabs over one round bamboo handle and sew ends together 1/2" up from bottom edges of tabs.

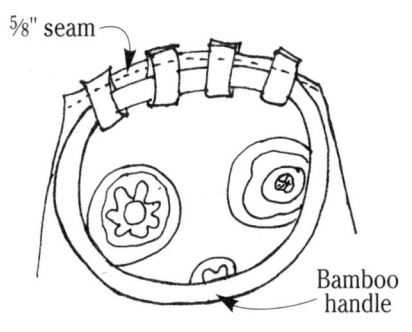

- 5/8" seam
- Bamboo handle

9. Pin tabs of handle to top outside of purse front. Do the same with the second handle on the back piece of the purse.
10. **Finishing top edges:** Clip curves on all 4 top edges of purse.
11. Turn in raw edges of purse front and back and lining. Topstitch front of purse from dot across top edge and back down to dot. Repeat on the back of the purse.

Fabric Bracelets

photos on pages 6 & 7

SIZE: To fit your wrist

FOR EACH BRACELET:
10" x 10" of each print
Black elastic thread (3 times your wrist measurement)
Fistful of Polyfil stuffing
16-20 plastic 3/4" curtain rings
4 large Orange plastic beads for Orange bracelet
Sharp needle with large eye

ASSEMBLY:
1. Make 6-8 round beads: 2" circles made into yo-yo's and stuffed with poly-fil. Make 16-20 flat beads: 2" circles with 3/4" plastic curtain rings inside of yo-yo.
2. Measure your wrist. Cut elastic thread 3 x the length of your wrist measurement.
3. Thread needle with elastic thread and string the stuffed yo-yo's into a bracelet with a flat bead between each yo-yo.
4. Go through bracelet twice with elastic thread. Pull elastic tightly and tie off. Trim ends of elastic to 1/4".

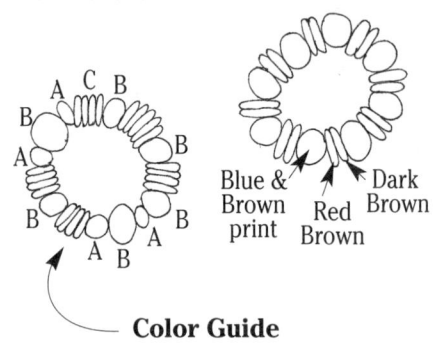

Blue & Brown print — Red Brown — Dark Brown

Color Guide

A - Purchased bead
B - Orange print stuffed bead
C - Variety of coordinating prints - all flat beads

Citrus Fun Shoes

photo is on page 6

MATERIALS:
Canvas shoes
Scraps of fabric
Assorted buttons
6 strand embroidery floss
Sewing machine, needle, thread
AccuQuilt® GO!™ Fabric Cutter (#55100)
  GO! Die circles 2", 3", 5" (#55012)

ASSEMBLY:
1. See diagrams for size of fabric circle to make yo-yo's and placement.
2. Using all 6 strands of floss, stack yo-yo's and buttons in desired order.

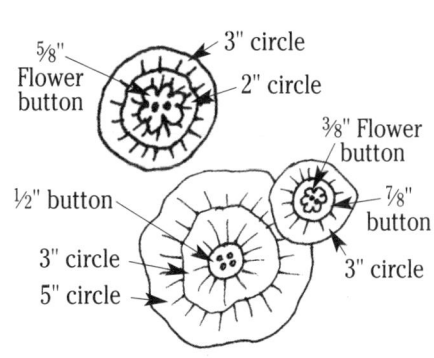

- 5/8" Flower button
- 3" circle
- 2" circle
- 3/8" Flower button
- 1/2" button
- 7/8" button
- 3" circle
- 3" circle
- 5" circle

3. Go in from top of button, down through yo-yo and come out inside shoe. Go back up through yo-yo and button. Pull threads tight and tie 3 knots. Cut off excess thread close to knots.

14 Wearables on the GO!

Bottle Cap Necklace

photo is on page 7

SIZE: 24"

YARDAGE:
Scraps (Lt. Green, Med Green, Orange, Gold, Red)
28" Black 2mm Tubing
Spring closures with lobster claw clasp
6 washers 1¼" wide
6 plastic rings ¾" wide
6 plastic water bottle caps
AccuQuilt® GO!™ Fabric Cutter (#55100)
  GO! Die Circles 2", 3", 5" (#55012)

ASSEMBLY:
1. Cut 4 Lt. Green and 2 Red 2" circles for ring yo-yos.
2. Cut 4 Orange and 2 Gold 3" circles for bottle cap yo-yos.
3. Cut 4 Gold and 2 Med Green 3" circles for washer yo-yos.
4. Arrange 2 sets: Lt Green ring-Orange cap-2 Gold washers-Orange cap-Lt Green ring. These will be on each side of the center. 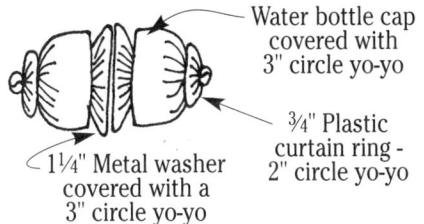
5. Arrange 1 set: Red ring-Gold cap-2 Dk Green washers-Gold cap-Red ring.
6. Follow diagrams for stringing and knotting of necklace parts.
7. Attach clasp.

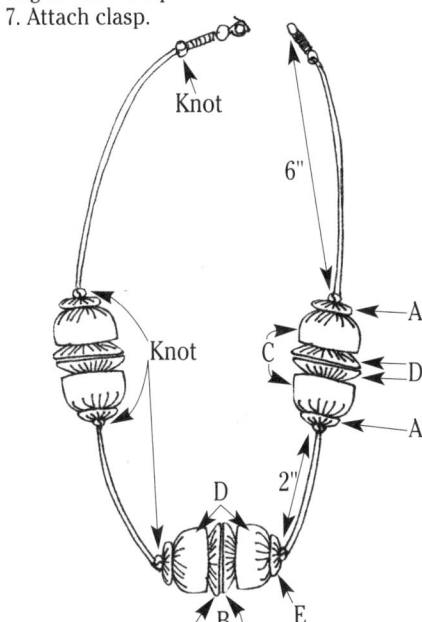

Color Guide for Prints
A - Lt Green
B - Med Green
C - Orange
D - Gold
E - Red

Thread Spool & Bead Necklace

photo is on page 7

SIZE: 32"

YARDAGE:
5" x 7" Scraps of 2 different prints (Gold, Red)
40" Black 2mm tubing
Spring closures with lobster claw clasp
One empty 1¼" wide x 1¾" long thread spool
2 wood 1" x 1" beads with large holes.
Variegated 10M thread (Blue, Green)
Hot Fix Crystals (Blue, Orange)
Six ¾" plastic curtain rings
200 Green E-beads
Needle and thread
AccuQuilt® GO!™ Fabric Cutter (#55100)
  GO! Die Circles 2", 3", 5" (#55012)

ASSEMBLY:
1. **Wood beads:** Wrap 1 wood bead with Blue thread and the other with Green thread.
2. Decorate with crystals.
3. **Cutting:** Cut two 3" Gold circles and six 2" Red circles.
4. Cover each ¾" plastic ring with a yo-yo made out of a 2" circle.
5. Cover each end of the spool with a yo-yo made from a 3" circle.
6. Using the needle and heavy thread, tie thread to 1 end of the spool. String the E beads onto the needle and thread. Wrap the strings of beads around the spool, covering the spool. Fasten the thread securely to the other end of the spool.
7. See Necklace Assembly Guide for threading beads and knot placement. Adjust length to personal preference and add closure parts.

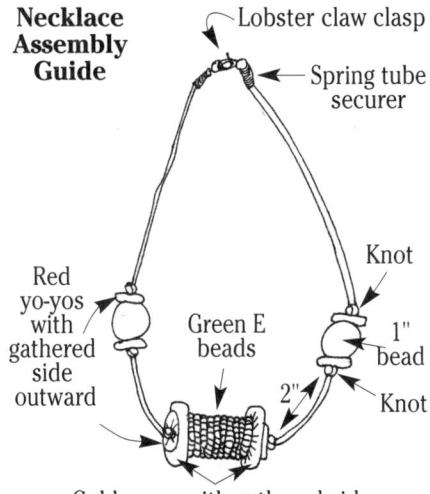

Yo-Yos & Bobbins Bracelet

photo is on page 7

SIZE: to fit your wrist

YARDAGE:
5" x 7" scraps of knit and woven fabrics
1 oz. polyfil
24" Black elastic thread
7 metal sewing machine bobbins
150 Green E-beads
Needle and heavy Black thread
AccuQuilt® GO!™ Fabric Cutter (#55100)
  GO! Die #55012 Circle – 2", 3", 5"

ASSEMBLY:
1. **Bobbin Beads:** Die cut two 2" circles, in matching colors, for each bobbin.
2. Sew one of the circles into a yo-yo. (See general instructions for "Making a Yo-Yo").
3. Before closing the yo-yo, place it over one side of the bobbin. Pull the gathering tight and secure with a knot. 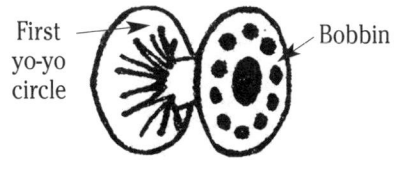
4. Do the same thing with the second yo-yo, but after securing the knot, do not cut off the needle and thread. 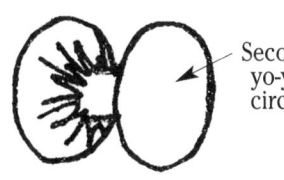
5. Feed enough beads onto the thread to circle the center of the bobbin. There should be no gaps between beads and it should fit tightly around the center. Secure thread.
Repeat for all remaining bobbins. 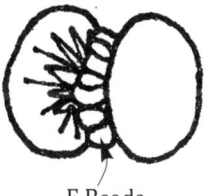
6. **Knit Beads:** Die cut seven 3" knit fabric circles. Sew each of them as yo-yos. (See general instructions for "Making a Yo-Yo"). Before closing the yo-yo, fill it with polyfil.
7. **Bracelet:** Measure your wrist. Cut elastic thread 3 times the length of your wrist measurement.
8. Thread needle with elastic thread and string the stuffed yo-yos into a bracelet with a bobbin between each yo-yo.
9. Go through bracelet twice with elastic thread. Pull elastic tightly and tie off. Trim ends of elastic to ¼".

Wearables on the GO! 15

Yo-Yo Necklace Variations

photo is on page 7
SIZE: 3 yo-yo pendant 4" long;
metal & yo-yo pendant 6" long
SUPPLIES:
3 Large yo-yos made from 5" circles
3 Medium yo-yos made from 3" circles
4 Small yo-yos made from 2" circles
Flat disks (one 1 3/4", three 7/8")
2 jump rings 1/4" each
Neck Chain, cord or metal neck ring
Decorative hardware
Button
E-bead
Needle and thread
ASSEMBLY:
1. See Yo-Yo General Instructions for making yo-yos. Place a 7/8" disk inside each 2" yo-yo to keep them flat and provide weight.

2. **3 Yo-Yo Pendant:** Sew a 3" yo-yo to each side of the 5" yo-yo. Sew a 2" yo-yo to each side of the 3" yo-yo.
3. Sew the yo-yos together: 2"-3"-5".

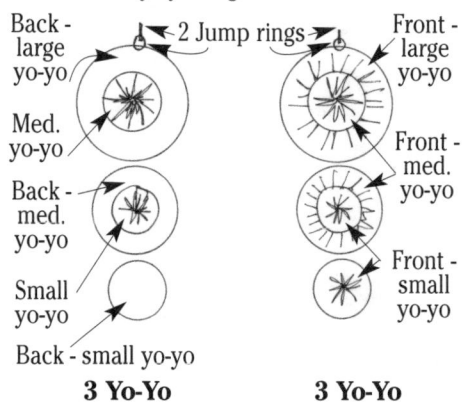

3 Yo-Yo Pendant Front Assembly
- Back - large yo-yo
- 2 Jump rings
- Med. yo-yo
- Back - med. yo-yo
- Small yo-yo
- Back - small yo-yo

3 Yo-Yo Pendant Back Assembly
- Front - large yo-yo
- Front - med. yo-yo
- Front - small yo-yo

4. **Metal & Yo-Yo Pendant:** Sew two 5" yo-yos with flat sides together. On one side, sew a 2" yo-yo and an E-bead over the center. On the other side, attach a decorative button. Attach metal loops and decorative hardware.
5. Sew a jump ring to the top of the yo-yo.
6. Attach to chain, cord or neck ring with a jump ring.

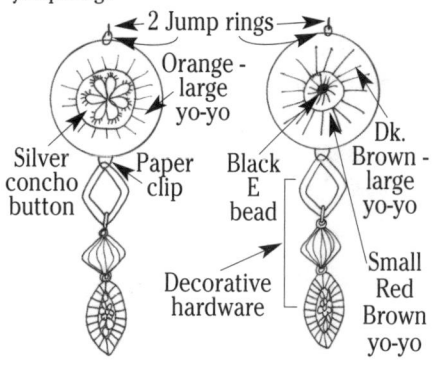

Metal & Yo-Yo Pendant Front Assembly
- 2 Jump rings
- Orange - large yo-yo
- Silver concho button
- Paper clip
- Decorative hardware

Metal & Yo-Yo Pendant Back Assembly
- Black E bead
- Dk. Brown - large yo-yo
- Small Red Brown yo-yo

Round Heart Purse

photo is on page 8
SIZE: 17" x 17"
YARDAGE:
I used *Henry Glass & Co.* "Opulence" by Brenda Pinnick
   1 1/8 yd x 45" each of 2 prints for hearts, button and handle tables
Purchase a pattern with a flat front at least 16" x 16"
Other yardage and notions requirements on purchased pattern
Four paintable wooden napkin rings
Acrylic Paints (Gold, Red, Lt Blue, Dk Blue, Yellow, Toffee)
Large hole 1 1/2" disks (4 Dark Blue, 4 Mustard)
8 hammered Silver 1" disks
Brown leather handles with Silver rings
1 half ball covered 2 1/2" button
AccuQuilt® GO!™ Fabric Cutter (#55100)
   GO! Die Hearts 2", 3", 4" (#55029)
ASSEMBLY:
1. Construct bag according to purchased pattern instructions.
2. **Substitute Handles:** Refer to the Handles Diagram.
3. **Hearts:** Die cut 50 plaid and 62 floral 4" hearts. With right sides together, sew 25 plaid hearts and 31 floral hearts. Leave the bottom of all hearts open for turning. Clip center of heart and turn right side out.

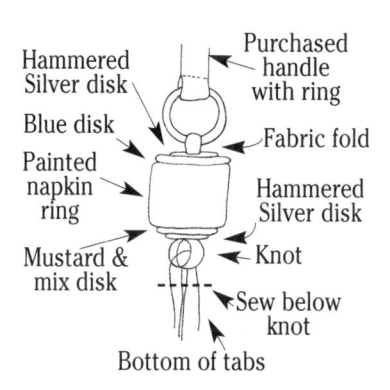

Handles Diagram
- Hammered Silver disk
- Purchased handle with ring
- Blue disk
- Fabric fold
- Painted napkin ring
- Hammered Silver disk
- Mustard & mix disk
- Knot
- Sew below knot
- Bottom of tabs

4. Pin hearts in place while assembling rows. Start with a center of 4 plaid hearts, next row 6 floral, 8 plaid, 10 floral, 13 plaid, 15 floral.
5. Using hand stitches, sew all hearts to bag.
6. Following manufacturer's instructions, cover ball button with floral fabric. Sew button securely to bag by hand-sewing the edges of the button fabric to the center of flower.

Strip Purse with Yoke Patterns
photo on page 9
instructions on page 18

**Strip Purse with Yoke
Pattern #4 - Flap Stabilizer**
Enlarge to 230%
Cut 1

**Strip Purse with Yoke
Pattern #2 - Purse Flap**
Enlarge to 230%
Cut 2

Wearables on the GO!

Stacked Layers Bag

photo is on page 8

SIZE: 13" x 15"

YARDAGE:
I used *Henry Glass & Co.* "Opulence" by Brenda Pinnick
1 yd of 45" wide fabric each of 2 contrasting prints and 1 yd each 6 solid coordinating colors
Straight pins
Sewing machine, needle, thread
4 tortoise shell napkin rings
Eight $2\frac{1}{2}$" tortoise shell rings with 1" openings
16 assorted 1" buttons
Yellow embroidery floss for sewing on buttons
AccuQuilt® GO!™ Fabric Cutter (#55100)
   GO! Die $2\frac{1}{2}$" strip cutter (#55017)

ASSEMBLY:
1. Lay one of the 1 yd prints face down on a flat surface. Stack the solid 1 yd cuts, wrong side up, on top of the print. Place the second print, right side up, on top of the stack.
2. Pin the layers together, approximately every 2".
3. Using the sewing machine and contrasting sewing thread, sew the sandwich of fabric together, with free motion designs, until you have removed all of the straight pins and the sandwich is now one piece of quilted fabric.
4. **Cutting:** Die cut the following strips:
   16 Purse Sides   18" x $2\frac{1}{2}$"
   2 Purse Handles   40" x $2\frac{1}{2}$"
   4 Purse Handle Stays   8" x $2\frac{1}{2}$"
   1 inside pocket   10" x 6"
   1 one bottom from pattern
5. **Sewing:** Sew all 16 strips together with $\frac{1}{2}$" seams and again with $\frac{3}{8}$" seams. Alternate prints. The raw edges will be on the outside. Leave the last seam open. 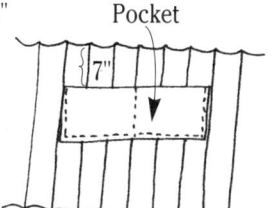
6. Even up the top and bottom of purse side to 17".
7. Sew around edges of pocket, $\frac{1}{2}$" from edge and again $\frac{3}{8}$" from edge.
8. Pin pocket to inside of bag, 7" down from top edge.
9. Sew sides and bottom of pocket. Sew down the center of the pocket, forming 2 pockets.
10. Sew last seam of bag sides together.
11. Sew the bottom of the bag to end of tube, with the raw edges on the outside. Make sure the pocket openings are facing the open end (top) of the bag.
12. Fold down $2\frac{1}{2}$" of the top of the purse. The folded down portion should be on the outside of the purse.
13. Fold the $2\frac{1}{2}$" wide strips (used for the straps and the handle stays) in half the long way, forming two $1\frac{1}{4}$" x 40" and four $1\frac{1}{4}$" x 8" straps. Sew down the raw edge side $\frac{1}{2}$" from edge and again $\frac{3}{8}$" from edge. 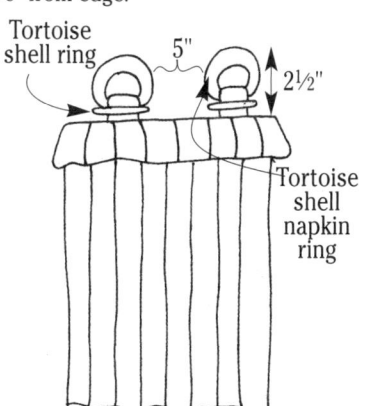
14. Thread one of the short pieces through a napkin ring, even up the ends and push both ends through one of the tortoise shell rings. Sew the raw ends to the inside of the purse, 5" apart, with 2" of the folded strip above the folded edge.
15. Push each end of the handle strips through a tortoise shell ring, then through the napkin ring and back through the tortoise shell ring. Sew the ends of the handles on the inside of the handle.
16. Using 6 strands of floss, sew on buttons to each of the strips that were folded over at the top of the purse.

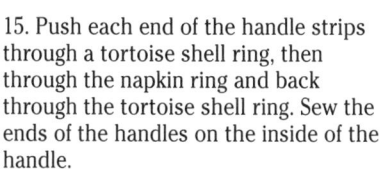

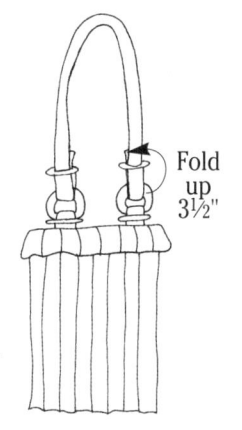

Purse Bottom Pattern
Enlarge to 235%

Pocket

Strip Purse with Yoke Patterns
instructions on page 18

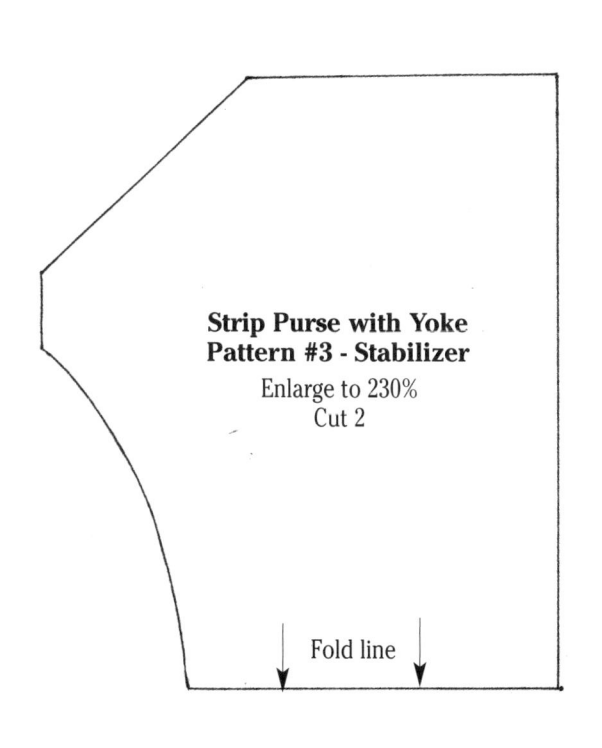

Strip Purse with Yoke Pattern #3 - Stabilizer
Enlarge to 230%
Cut 2

Fold line

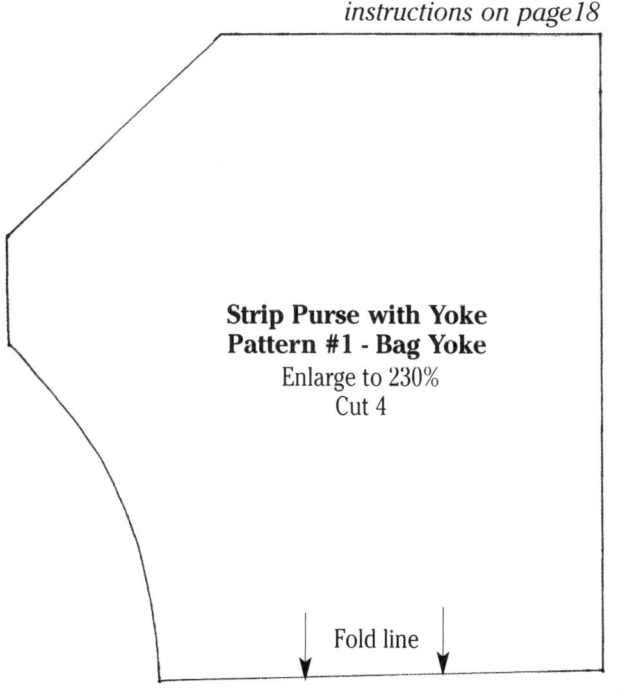

Strip Purse with Yoke Pattern #1 - Bag Yoke
Enlarge to 230%
Cut 4

Fold line

Strip Purse with Yoke

photo is on page 9

SIZE: 18" x 18" not counting handles
YARDAGE:
I used Clothworks "Piccadilly" by Pamela Mostek
Choose 7 coordinating prints:
  6 prints   10" x 45" for strips only
  1 print   ½ yd x 45" for lining and pocket
  1 print   1 yd x 45" for 2 strips, yokes, closure flap, 4 strap tabs
37" x 20" Super heavy weight stabilizer
1 magnetic purse closure
2 Silver 1½" rings
Silver 16½" chain link handles
16 yds Brown Maxi piping
Sewing machine, needle, thread
AccuQuilt® GO!™ Fabric Cutter (#55100)
  GO! Die 2½" strip cutter (#55017)

ASSEMBLY:
1. **Fabric Cutting:** Cut fourteen 2½" x 32" strips – 2 of each of the 7 coordinating prints
   1 lining 15½" x 23"
   2 pocket pieces 6" x 10" from same fabric as lining
   4 purse yokes from coordinating print – Pattern #1
   2 closure flap pieces (same fabric as purse yoke) Pattern #2
   1 multi-colored 2½" x 32" strip for flower on closure
   4 handle tabs 4" x 6" using same fabric as purse yoke
2. **Stabilizer:** Cut 1 piece 14½" wide x 22½" long for lining
   2 for yokes using Pattern #3
   1 for purse flap using Pattern #4
   4 pieces 1" x 6" for handle tabs
3. **Bag Base:** Lay out strips in order 1-7.
4. Sew a strip of piping on the right side of the fabric, along right edge of the strips, with the raw edges of the piping along the right edge of the strips. 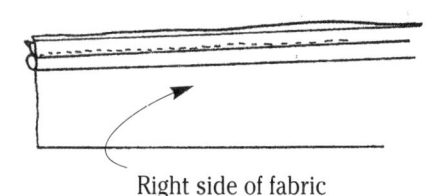
5. After piping is added to all of the strips, join the strips together as follows. With right sides together, sew the second strip to the first, as close to the piping as possible. Open up and repeat process until you have 14 strips with piping between them to form bag fabric. Add one last piece of piping to the left side of strip #1 so that there is piping on both sides of the constructed fabric.
6. With right sides together, sew the side seams, leaving 3" free at top of bag on each side. 
7. **Pocket:** With right sides together, sew around edges of pocket pieces, leaving an opening on the bottom edge for turning. Turn to right side and close opening.
8. Center pocket 2" from top edge of lining and sew pocket to inside of lining.
9. Sew a seam down the pocket to divide it into two pockets. 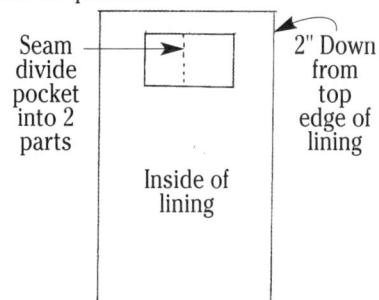
10. Fold lining in half, with the right sides together, and sew side seams. Stop sewing 3" from top of lining on both sides.
11. Fold in raw edges of lining ½" and raw edges of bag.
12. Sew a Gathering stitch along each of the top edges of the bag. Pull them to match up with the top edges of the lining. Sew both sides of bag, along the top edge, to top edges of lining.
13. Sew down openings on either side, joining lining to bag sides. 
14. **Yoke:** Sew piping to the bottom of the right side of two of the yoke pieces. Raw edges of piping should match up with the raw edges of the bottom of the yoke. 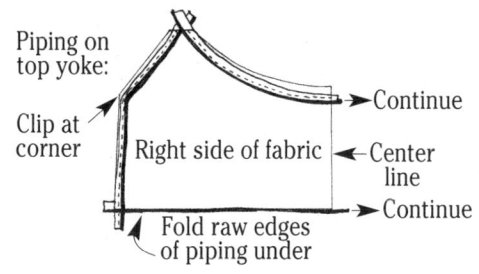
15. Fold raw edges of bottom of yoke to the wrong side of the yoke and sew piping along all remaining edges of the yoke, except across the two points where the rings will be attached.
16. **Ring Tabs:** Fold each of the four handle tabs in half with right sides together and sew a ⅝" seam down the 6" sides. Turn to right side and press. 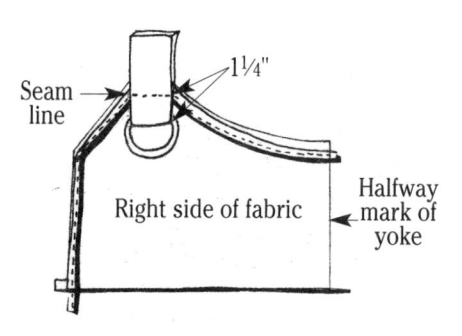
17. Insert one stabilizer piece into each of the tabs. Fold each tab through a metal ring and even up the ends. Sew to right side of yokes.
18. **Closure Flap:** Sew piping around all sides of one of the closure flaps, on the right side of the fabric. Do not sew piping on the straight top edge.
19. With right sides together, sew both pieces of closure flap together. Leave the straight top edge open. Turn to right side, press and insert stabilizer. Sew across straight end.
20. Add ½ of magnetic closure to curved end of flap, approximately 1" in from edge.
21. **Finish Yokes:** With right sides together, sew all around yoke, leaving bottom edge open. Turn to right side.
22. **Sew Flap to Bag:** With raw edges of flap centered on the outside upper raw edge of bag back, sew to bag. 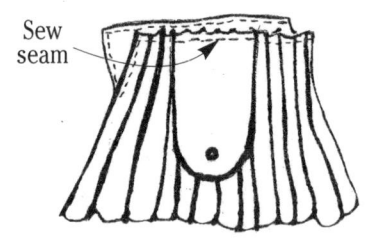
23. Add yoke to bag by lining up right sides of yokes with top right sides of bag and sewing them together. 
24. Insert yoke stabilizer, turn under raw edges of inside of yoke and hand sew them to the lining side of the bag.
25. Add handles and other half of magnetic closure to front yoke.
26. **Flower Decoration:** (Covers magnetic closure) With right sides together, sew a 2½" x 32" multi-colored strip down the long sides, using a ½" seam. Turn to right side. Press. Turn in raw ends.
27. Sew a gathering cord along one side and gather the tube.
Starting at one end, hand-sew the tube into a tight spiral. Keep winding the spiral, as you sew it to the previous spiral, to from a rose. Sew rose over magnetic closure.

Wearables on the GO!

Copper Fleece Rag Square Scarf

photo is on page 28
SIZE: 6" x 70"
YARDAGE: 1 yd fleece
Sewing machine, needle, thread
AccuQuilt® GO!™ Fabric Cutter (#55100)
  GO! Die Rag Square 5¼" (#55033)

ASSEMBLY:
1. Die cut 33 Rag Squares.
2. Fold each square into a triangle, with the bottom fringe just below the top fringe

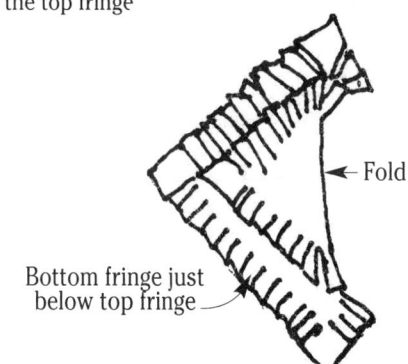

3. Stack triangles, with each triangle's fringe just below the previous triangle.
4. Sew down the center.

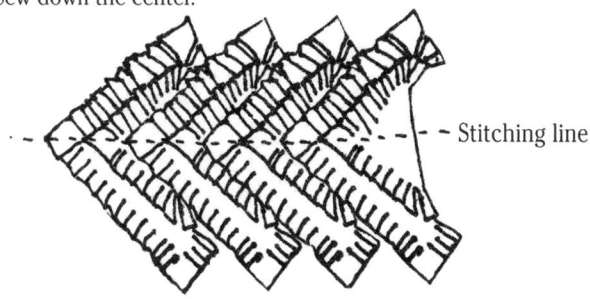

Rag Square Scarves

photo is on pages 28 - 29
SIZE: 6" x 100"
YARDAGE:
Red wool felt from recycled sweaters or 1 yard fleece
Sewing machine, needle, thread
AccuQuilt® GO!™ Fabric Cutter (#55100)
  GO! Die Rag Square 5¼" (#55033)

ASSEMBLY:
1. Felting sweaters: Choose 100% wool sweaters from a thrift store. Wash in a washing machine with detergent and hot water. Dry in hot dryer. If you want a tighter felt, repeat process.
2. Die cut 31 squares of wool or fleece.
3. Arrange squares on the diagonal, overlapping so the corner of the upper square meets the center of the previous square.
4. Sew the squares down the center.

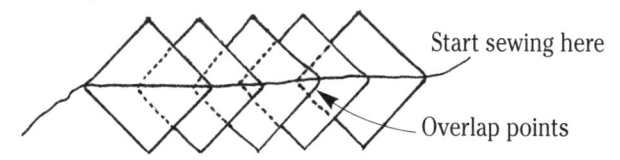

Dotted line indicated bottom points

5. Fluff fringes by throwing scarf in the dryer for 15 minutes.

Large Rag Square Stretch Scarf

photo is on page 28
SIZE: 4" x 55"
YARDAGE:
1 yd x 42" each – Macaw Red and Coral Reef Bamboo felt
55" round cord elastic
Sewing machine, needle, thread
AccuQuilt® GO!™ Fabric Cutter (#55100)
  GO! Die 8½" Rag Square (#55013)

ASSEMBLY:
1. Die cut 12 Rag Squares from each of the two colors of felt.
2. Overlap squares as in diagram and sew until all squares are joined.

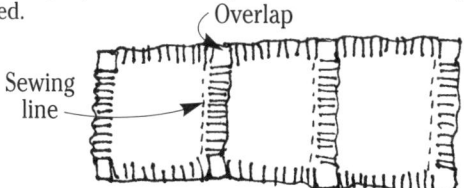

3. Fold the scarf in half lengthwise and sew down folded edge ½" from edge of fold.
4. Run elastic through the sewn tube and secure at each end with a knot in the elastic and then sew the knot in place.

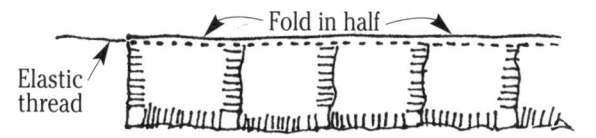

5. Wash the bamboo scarf and dry for just a few minutes in the dryer.
6. Remove from the dryer and block the still damp scarf by pinning it open on a flat surface.

Giraffe Print Rag Square Scarf

photo is on page 29
SIZE: 5¼" x 100"
YARDAGE:
1 yard Giraffe fleece
Sewing machine, needle, thread
AccuQuilt® GO!™ Fabric Cutter (#55100)
  GO! Die Rag Square 5¼" (#55033)

ASSEMBLY:
1. Die cut 30 squares.
2. Overlap squares, with 1st square's fringe overlapping 2nd square, so that the squares meet just above the fringes.

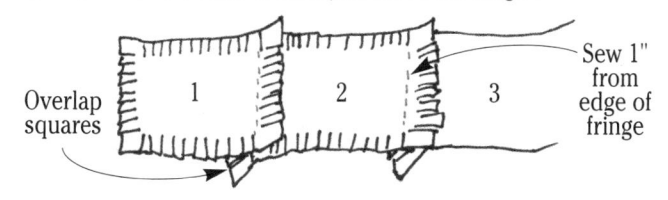

3. Sew across overlapping fringes, 1" from edge of top fringe, which should be just on the solid area of the square, just above the fringe.
4. Continue until desired length is reached.

Wearables on the GO! 19

Gathered Rag Square Boa Scarf

photo is on page 28

SIZE: Pink - 4" x 60"; Earthtone - 4" x 75"

YARDAGE:
1/3 yd x 60" each of 5 Earthtone fleece prints
2/3 yd each of Pink and Green fleece
1 skein *DMC* pearl cotton #5 (complimentary color)
Needle and heavy duty sewing thread
AccuQuilt® GO!™ Fabric Cutter (#55100)
   GO! Die Rag Square 5 1/4" (#55033)

ASSEMBLY:
1. Die cut 20 Rag Squares from each of the 5 Earthtone colors.
2. Die cut 37 Pink and 38 Green Rag Squares for the Pink/Green boa.
3. With double thread, hand-sew in a 2" circle in the center of each square.

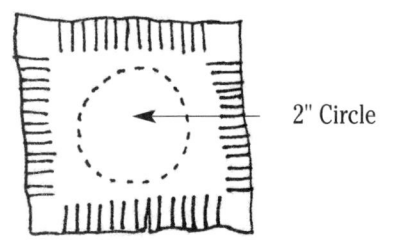

2" Circle

4. Gather it very tightly and secure the thread. Repeat for all squares.

Gathered circle

5. For Earthtone boa, number the colors 1-5 to keep the same pattern throughout the scarf. For Pink Green boa, alternate the colors. Using pearl cotton, sew the squares together at the gathering line to form a long string of gathered squares.
6. Give the scarf a few twists and the squares will fan out into a boa.

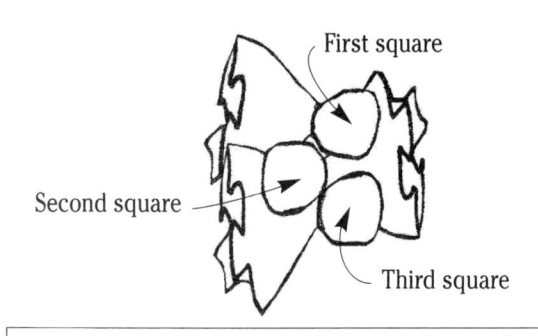

First square
Second square
Third square

Brown & Black Rag Square Scarf

photo is on page 29

SIZE: 5 1/4" x 60"

YARDAGE:
1/2 yd x 60" fleece (Brown, Black)
Sewing machine, needle, thread
AccuQuilt® GO!™ Fabric Cutter (#55100)
   GO! Die Rag Square 5 1/4" (#55033)

ASSEMBLY:
1. Cut 28 Black and 29 Brown rag squares.
2. Starting with a Brown square, alternate Brown and Black squares.
3. Fold the first Brown square in half.

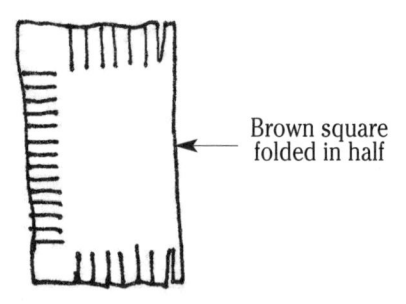

Brown square folded in half

4. Fold the second square over the 1st, so that edges of second square start just above the fringe of the first square.

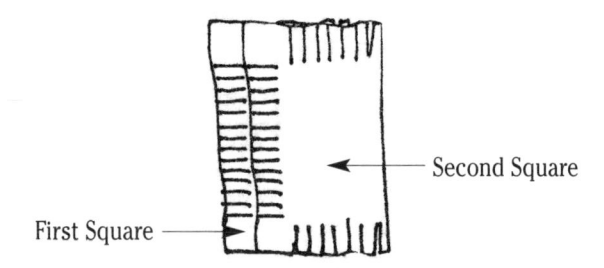

Second Square
First Square

5. Sew across the second square just above 2nd fringe.

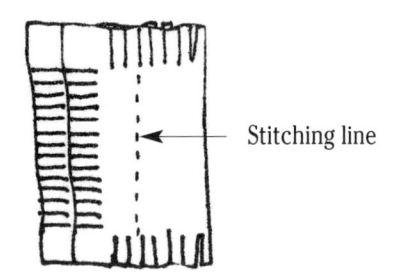

Stitching line

6. Continue overlapping squares and stitching, ending with a Brown square.

55 Circle Scarf

photo is on page 29

SIZE: 5 1/2" x 62"

YARDAGE:
24" of 40" wide soft Bamboo felt (Black, Gray)
Sewing machine, needle, thread
AccuQuilt® GO!™ Fabric Cutter (#55100)
   GO! Die Circle 2", 3", 5" (#55012)

ASSEMBLY:
1. Die cut 5" circles: 28 Black and 27 Gray.
2. Lay circles in a layered line, beginning and ending with Black, leaving 1" of showing between circles.

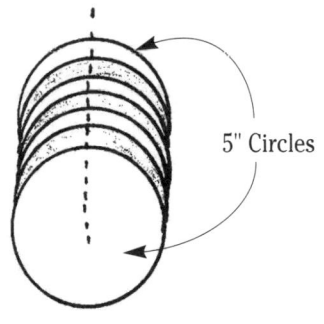

5" Circles

3. Pin circles in place.
4. Machine stitch straight down the center of the scarf.

20   *Wearables on the GO!*

Batik Jacket

photo is on pages 30 - 31

SIZE: Miss 12-14

Finished size depends on purchased pattern used.
Note: Size of created fabric depends on the fabric requirements of the chosen jacket pattern. My jacket required 3¼ yds of 45" fabric. I found that by cutting out the pattern pieces and fitting the created fabric to each piece resulted in the best use of the fabric.

YARDAGE:
Outside of jacket: 27" x 45" of 7 different Green/Brown batik prints
Lining: Brown batik as listed on the purchased pattern.
Heart trim: 2½ yds of same Brown batik used for jacket lining.
Interfacing: See purchased pattern for amount
Sewing machine, needle, thread
AccuQuilt® GO!™ Fabric Cutter (#55100)
    GO! Die 1½" strip cutter (#55024)
    GO! Die Hearts 2", 3", 4" (#55029)

ASSEMBLY:
1. **Outside of Jacket:** Cut the Green/Brown batik into strips 1½" x width of fabric. Keep the like strips together, so that you have 7 groups of strips.
2. Sew the strips together lengthwise, using a ½" seam in this order – 1,2,3,4,5,6,7 – 1,2,3,4,5,6,7. Repeat this pattern until you have the required size of fabric needed for the pattern pieces. 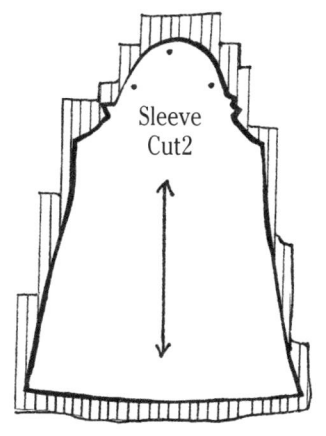
3. **Heart Trim:** Die cut 144 Brown 4" hearts for jacket edging. Die cut 60 Brown 3" hearts for sleeve edgings.

4. With right sides together, sew two hearts together around the outside, using a ¼" seam. Clip at center top of heart and cut a small slit, for turning to right side, in the center of one side only. Turn hearts to right side and press.

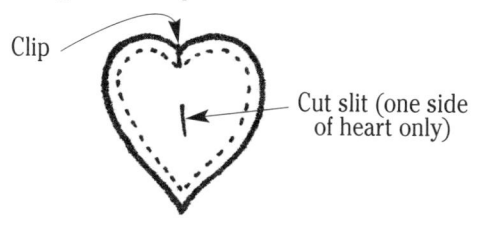

5. **Jacket Assembly:** Sew jacket together using the purchased pattern instructions.
6. **Sleeve Trim:** Using 3" hearts, arrange hearts with the bottom of one overlapping the top of previous heart. Be sure the slit sides are on the underside. Pin in place. 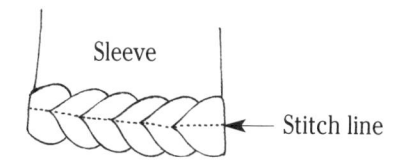
7. Sew along the centers of the hearts.
8: **Jacket Trim:** Starting at the back center bottom of jacket, and making sure all slit sides of hearts are on the underside, stitch hearts to edge of jacket. The center back hearts at top and bottom of jacket will be upside down. 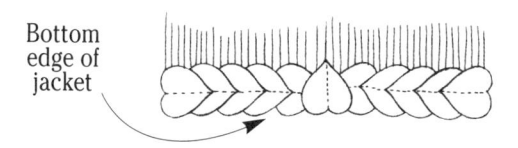
9. With needle and thread, tack the side edges of the hearts that overlap the jacket fabric to the jacket, so they remain flat when wearing the jacket.

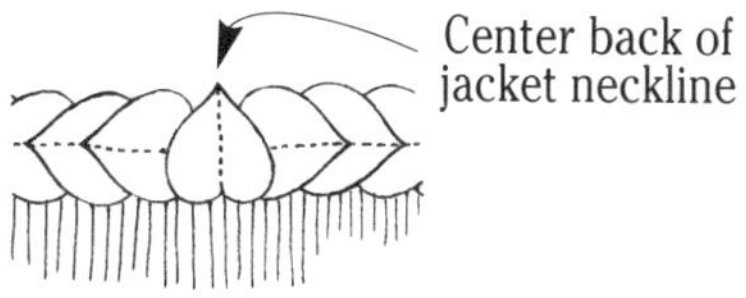

Distressed Leather Purse

photo is on pages 30 - 31

SIZE: 18" tall x 24" wide at bottom
YARDAGE:
½ yd x 30" Green-Brown batik fabric (piping)
7 yds cording to make piping
1½ yd x 45" distressed leather fabric
½ yd x 45" heavy fabric for lining and pocket
1 Brighton belt
2 Silver purse clasps
4 Silver 1½" diameter rings
4 Silver 2" swivel clips
8 yds of ⅛" cording
Sewing machine, needle, thread
AccuQuilt® GO!™ Fabric Cutter (#55100)
    GO! Die 1½" strip cutter (#55024)
    GO! Die 2½" strip cutter (#55017)

ASSEMBLY:
1. Refer to the Strip Purse instructions on page 18. Same construction as Strip Purse, with the following changes:
    All 2½" strips are cut from distressed leather fabric.
2. Cut batik into 1½" strips to make piping. Piping is used on every other strip to form the bag fabric.
3. **Handles:** Cut six 2½" x 32" strips of leather fabric. Cut 4 leather strips 3½" long x 5¾" wide for handle covers.
4. On all six 2½" x 32" strips, fold each strip lengthwise, right sides together and sew long seams to make a tube. Turn right side out.
5. Braid 3 strips together for each strap.
6. Pull ends through swivel clips and back around. Secure with needle and thread. Make sure both handles are the same length. 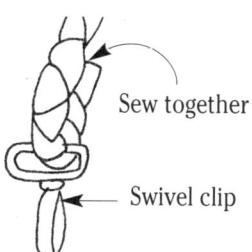
7. With right sides together, sew 3½" seams in handle covers. Turn to right side and slide over handles to cover raw edges of braid. Turn in raw edges and hand-sew in place at ends. Hook handles to purse.
8. Use parts of belt to embellish flap.

Wearables on the GO! 21

Pillow Case Child's Dress

photo is on page 34

SIZE: Child Size 6

Tip: For different sizes, use fewer or more strips. Also adjust length of strips as needed.

YARDAGE:
I used *Clothworks* "Baby Buggies" by Sue Zipkin
   10" x 30" of 10 different coordinating prints
   Scraps for applique: 5" x 5" Yellow, 2" x 2" Pink, 1" x 1" Green
56" grosgrain $1/8$" wide ribbon
1 pkg hem tape
$1\frac{1}{2}$ yd single fold wide bias tape
Sewing machine, needle, thread
AccuQuilt® GO!™ Fabric Cutter (#55100)
   GO! Die $2\frac{1}{2}$" strip cutter (#55017)

ASSEMBLY:
1. Cut all fabric into $2\frac{1}{2}$" x 30" strips for a total of 30 strips.
2. Arrange fabric as desired.
3. With right sides together, using $1/2$" seams, sew the strips into a new piece of fabric.
4. Sew along the 30" lengths, in the arranged order until all strips are connected into a flat piece of fabric.
5. Turn fabric face down on ironing surface and press the seams open.
6. On the right side of the fabric, Topstitch $1/4$" from seams on both sides of the seams, using a thread that blends with the fabric.
7. Sew the last seam together to form a tube of fabric. Press the seam open and Topstitch on both sides of the seam.
8. Lay fabric tube on a flat surface and cut out the arm openings following the Arm Opening Cutting Pattern.
9. Fold bias tape over arm opening and Topstitch along edge of tape. See diagram.
10. Fold down 2" at top to the inside, turn under $1/4$" of raw edge and sew along the bottom edge, forming a tube for the ribbon ties. Cut ribbon in half, shape ends and run through the ribbon tubes. When wearing dress, pull ribbon ends to gather top edges of dress and tie a bow on each shoulder.
11. Sew hem tape to bottom edge of dress. Fold under hem and stitch hem by hand.
12. Cut a large flower, middle flower and flower center from fabric scraps and applique to front of dress.
13. As a variation, sew strips horizontally or use $1/4$" seams to make wider strips.

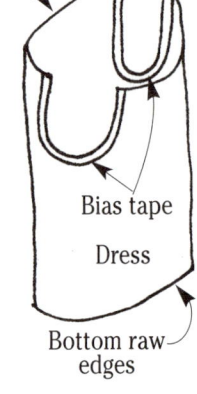

Arm Opening Cutting Pattern
Enlarge to 145%

Top of dress material
Cutting line
Place on fold line of top side of tube

Top raw edges
Bias tape
Dress
Bottom raw edges

Stitch Guide

Lazy Daisy
This stitch can stand-alone or be worked in a group to form a flower. You will come up at 1, form a loop, then go down at 2. Do not pull this thread tight, leave it in the loop shape, then come up at 3 and go down at 4 to tie the stitch down. You can vary the size of the loop or length to suit yourself! It can be small or large; there is no right or wrong size!

Lazy Daisy Stitch

Yoke Dress

photo is on page 35

SIZE: Child's 6

YARDAGE:
I used *Henry Glass & Co.* "Opulence" by Brenda Pinnick
   $1/2$ yd each of 10 prints
Purchase pattern with yoke
Any notions called for on pattern
Sewing machine, needle, thread
AccuQuilt® GO!™ Fabric Cutter (#55100)
   GO! Die $2\frac{1}{2}$" strip cutter (#55017)
   GO! Die circles 2", 3", 5" (#55012)

ASSEMBLY:
1. **Cutting:** Cut three $2\frac{1}{2}$" x 28" of each of the 10 prints.
   Cut yoke from one of the prints.
   Cut assortment of 2", 3", 5" circles from remaining fabric.
2. **Create fabric:** With right sides together, sew as many strips together as needed, using $1/2$" seams. (I needed 27 strips.)
3. Press seams open and Topstitch $1/2$" on either side of each seam.
4. Cut bottom of dress from the above created fabric.
5. Follow instructions for assembling dress according to pattern.
6. Make yo-yos from all of the circles.
7. Cover the yoke with combinations of 1, 2 or 3 yo-yo stacks.
8. Scatter a few yo-yo combinations on skirt.

Strap Dress

photo is on page 35

SIZE: Girl's 12-14

YARDAGE:
I used *Robert Kaufman* "Glam Garden" by Josephine Kimberling
$1/3$ yd x 45" each of 7 coordinating prints
30" elastic 1" wide
Sewing machine, needle, thread
AccuQuilt® GO!™ Fabric Cutter (#55100)
   GO! Die $2\frac{1}{2}$" strip cutter (#55017)

ASSEMBLY:
1. Cut all fabric into $2\frac{1}{2}$" x 45" strips.
2. Number prints 1-7 and, using $1/2$" seams, sew them together (strip 1 thru strip 7). After #7, repeat the order until the length is 4" shorter than the desired finished length. Desired length is measured from arm pit to desired length.
3. Press all seams downward and Topstitch $1/8$" from seam.
4. The hip measurement is 31". This dress is 42" around. The fabric strips are 46" long.

24 *Wearables on the GO!*

French Knot
Come up at 1, with the needle tip pointing toward your left arm, and wrap the thread twice around the needle. While holding the thread taut with your fingers, you want to turn the needle toward you, taking the needle down at 2, as close as you can to 1. You will want to slowly guide the thread into the fabric and hold the knot in place until your needle is all the way through the fabric.

French Knot

Chain Stitch
You will come up at 1 and go down at 2 then come up inside 2 for the 3rd stitch to shape your loop and go back down at 4 and continue till you reach the end of the area you want this to cover.

Chain Stitch

5. Cut off 4" across the strips to adjust to correct width.

Strap Dress

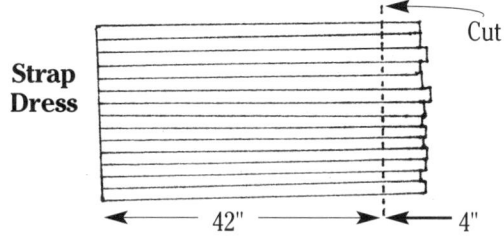

← 42" → ← 4" →

Cut

6. Sew the 4" strip to the bottom edge of the dress. You may need to create more strips to have enough to go across the bottom edge.

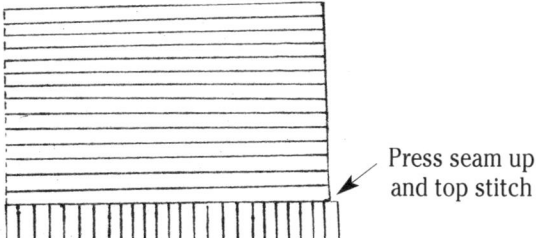

Press seam up and top stitch

7. Fold up raw edges and top stitch $1/8$" above seam.
8. With right sides together, sew back seam. Press and Topstitch.
9. Choose two $2 1/2$" x 45" strips. With right sides together, join these 2 strips of fabric to make the bottom ruffle. Hem the bottom.
10. Sew a Gathering thread along the top edge and gather.
11. With right sides together, pin the ruffle to the bottom of the dress. Press the seam upward and stitch $1/8$" from edge.
12. **Top of Dress:** Make a small opening in the seam of the top strip. Reinforce seam above and below the opening.
13. Fold the top strip over to the inside of the dress. Topstitch along top, $1/2$" down from the top.

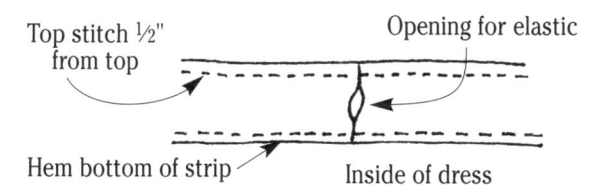

Top stitch $1/2$" from top
Opening for elastic
Hem bottom of strip
Inside of dress

14. Turn under bottom of strip and machine stitch closed.
15. Run 1" x desired length of elastic through the top of the dress. Close opening.
16. **Straps:** With right sides together, sew the long seam ($1/2$") on a $2 1/2$" x 45" strip. Turn to right side and cut in half. Press.
17. With dress on child, pin straps in place. Remove and sew straps to dress.

Wine Tote

photo is on page 9
SIZE: 5" x 5" x 15"
YARDAGE:
I used *Clothworks* "Piccadilly" by Pamela Mostek
   6" x 45" each of 5 coordinating prints
   12" x 45" of 2 coordinating solid cottons (Pink, Purple)
12" x 27" Nonwoven heavyweight interfacing
45" clothes line cord
4 Silver $3/8$" grommets and setting tool
Sewing machine, needle, thread
AccuQuilt® GO!™ Fabric Cutter (#55100)
   GO! Die $5 1/4$" Rag Square (#55033)
ASSEMBLY:
1. **Cutting:** Die cut 8 rag squares from each of 4 prints.
   Die cut 17 rag squares from each of the 2 solids.
   Cut 17 squares ($3 1/2$" x $3 1/2$") of heavyweight interfacing.
   From 5th print, cut 2 rag squares and a 2" x 45" strip.
2. Number the prints 1- 4.
3. **Stack** squares in this order: Stack one #1, face down, follow with 1 Pink, center interfacing, 1 Purple and a #1, face up. Do this with the remaining #1 prints. Then do the same with the #2's, #3's and #4's.
4. Free-motion sew through all layers of fabric-stacked squares.

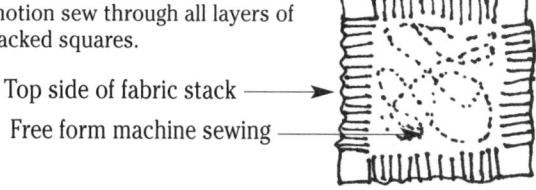

Top side of fabric stack
Free form machine sewing

5. Assemble the 17th square and free-motion sew through all layers.
6. Arrange squares into 4 strips of 4 squares each.

1	4	1	4
2	3	2	3
3	2	3	2
4	1	4	1

5

7. Sew them together with the fringes on the right side.
8. Sew the strips together to form a tube.
9. Apply grommets to opposite squares at top of wine holder, placing them 1" apart and $1/4$" down from beginning of fringe.
10. Sew square to bottom of holder.
11. With right sides together, fold 2" x 45" strip in half and sew a $1/4$" seam down long side. Turn to right side and run the clothes line through the tube. Cut the tube in half.
12. Push ends from outside to inside, through the grommets, to form a handle. Knot both ends of each handle. Add bottle of wine.

Diagonal Weave Bag
photo on page 27
instructions on page 26

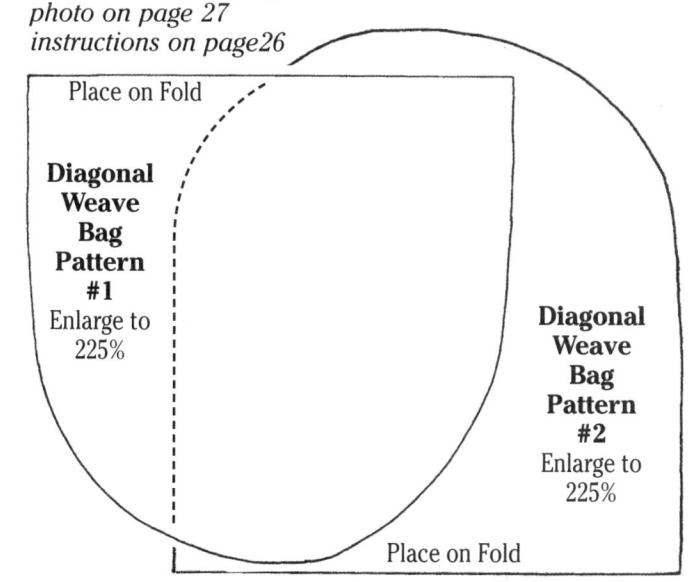

Place on Fold

Diagonal Weave Bag Pattern #1
Enlarge to 225%

Diagonal Weave Bag Pattern #2
Enlarge to 225%

Place on Fold

Wearables on the GO! 25

Diagonal Weave Bag

photo is on page 27

SIZE: 12" high x 11" wide

YARDAGE:
I used *Studio e Fabrics* "Road to Marrakech" by B J Lanz
  1/3 yd x 45" each of 12 variations of prints for outside of bag.
1/2 yd x 45" for lining and bag bottom
6" x 29" of 2 prints for handles
20"x 36" Sew-in medium weight non woven stabilizer
Straight pins
Sewing machine, needle, thread
AccuQuilt® GO!™ Fabric Cutter (#55100)
  GO! Die 2 1/2" strip cutter (#55017)
Corrugated cardboard to make a stack 23 1/2" around x 15" high
Craft glue

ASSEMBLY:
1. Glue the cardboard together and let dry.

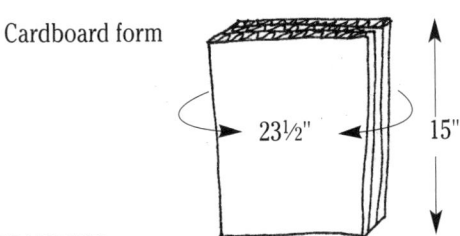

FROM FABRIC:
2. Cut 48 strips 2 1/2" x 36" (4 from each of the 12 prints for weaving).
3. Cut 4 handles 2 1/2" x 29" (2 strips from each of two different prints).
4. Use Pattern #1 to cut 2 bag bottoms and 2 bag bottom linings.
5. Cut 12" x 25" for lining.

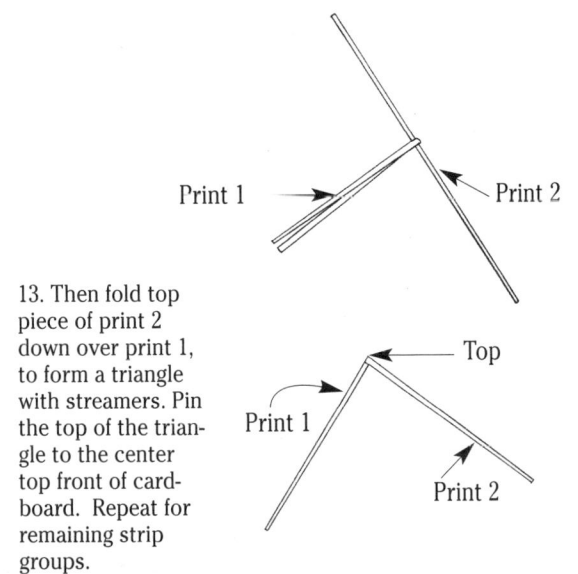

FROM STABILIZER:
6. Cut 2 pieces 6" x 10" for inside pocket (use any print).
7. Using Pattern #2, cut 1 bag bottom and 1 bag lining.
8. Cut two 7/8" x 29" pieces for handles.
9. Cut one 10" x 24 1/2" piece for bag lining.
10. **Weaving:** With right sides together, fold weaving strips in half lengthwise and using a 1/2" seam allowance, sew into tubes. Turn all tubes right side out and press flat with the seam on the back side of each strip. Separate the strips into prints and number 1-12.
11. Print 1 and 2, 3 and 4, 5 and 6, etc. will be used to form weaving strips.
12. Fold center of print 1 over center of print 2.
13. Then fold top piece of print 2 down over print 1, to form a triangle with streamers. Pin the top of the triangle to the center top front of cardboard. Repeat for remaining strip groups.
14. Pin, one at a time, to the top front of the cardboard, keeping each one tight up next to the previous one. Weave, as you go, with a simple over and under weave, using both ends of each strip as if it were one strip. 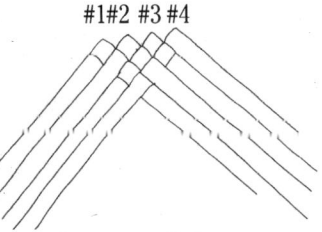
15. Continue pinning and weaving all the way around the block of cardboard. This forms one continuous piece. Keep weaves close together as you go.
16. Hand baste along bottom of weave. Remove pins and pull bag off of the cardboard. Machine stitch along bottom, 12" from top of bag (the pointed tip end is the top of the bag).
17. Trim off excess 3/4" below line of stitching. Remove basting threads. Note: Every bag will be different, so you may need to trim some off of your bag bottom to make it fit.
18. Bag bottom consists of stabilizer sandwiched between the two print pieces with their right sides facing out. Mark off center sides and middle centers to match up with bag.
19. Stitch just outside of stabilizer, which is smaller than the print fabric and may also need to be trimmed. 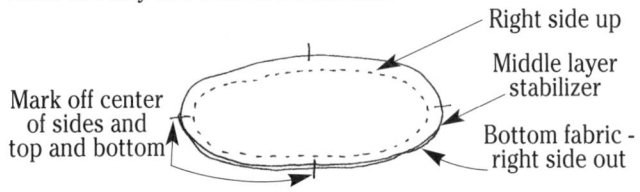
20. Turn the bag inside out. Match up sides and middle centers to bag bottom and sew together with raw edges exposed. Turn bag back to right side.
21. **Pocket:** With right sides together, sew all around pocket, leaving opening for turning. Turn, press and close opening. Sew to inside of lining 1 1/2" down from top edge of lining.
22. Sew a seam down the center of the pocket to form 2 pockets.
23. **Lining:** With right sides together, sew the 12" sides together. Create the lining bottom piece exactly like you did for the bottom of the bag, using two pieces of fabric and 1 piece of stabilizer.
24. Sew bottom to side of lining with raw edges on the wrong side.
25. Make a tube with the lining stabilizer. Overlap the 10" sides 1/2" and hand-sew the seam together.
26. Pull the lining up through the stabilizer tube. Fold the top over to the outside 1 1/4" and hand sew to stabilizer.
27. Add magnetic snaps. 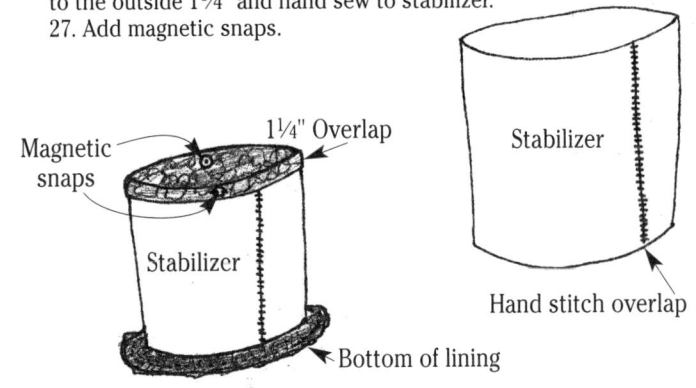
28. **Handles:** Use one print for the top of the handle and the second print for the bottom of the handle. With right sides together, sew a 5/8" seam down each side of the handles. Turn right side out and press both handles.
29. Insert stabilizer strips into the handles.
30. Attach handles to outside of lining stabilizer, 2" from top edge and 4 1/2" apart.
31. Insert lining into bag and sew top edge of lining to inside of bag approximately 3/4" down from top outside of bag.

26 *Wearables on the GO!*

Diagonal Weave Purse

Use up a dozen coordinating left-over prints with a fun project that makes a great gift. Basic under-over weaving techniques make this purse easy to accomplish.

instructions on page 26

Collapsible Koozie

photo is above

This handy collapsible container keeps drinks warm and will prevent a drink from leaving a ring on the table.

SIZE: 4" x 4" x 4"

YARDAGE:
5 Rag squares created the same as the squares for the small rag square purse (page 11)
5" *Velcro* sew-on tape $5/8$" wide
Hole punch, Two $3/8$" grommets with setting tool
One $4 1/4$" chain link with attached eyelet ends
$7/8$" buttons (1 Purple, 1 Green)
Handful of Poly-fil stuffing
Sewing machine, needle, thread
AccuQuilt® GO!™ Fabric Cutter (#55100)
   GO! Die Funky Flower (#55042)
   GO! Die Rag Square $5 1/4$" (#55033)

ASSEMBLY:
1. **Box:** Prepare 5 squares like rag squares for Rag Square Purse on page 11.
2. Sew the 5 squares together to form a box without a top. All fringe is on the outside of the box.

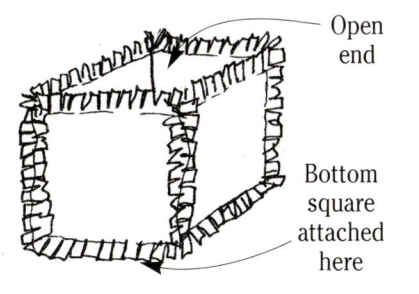

3. Leaving room for the Velcro in step 4, on two attached sides of the box, add a grommet and insert chain.

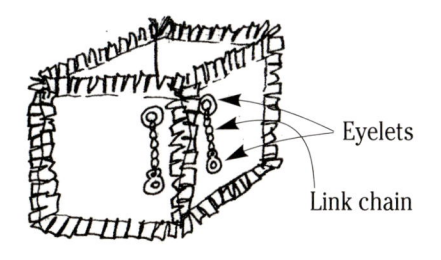

4. Cut 5" strip of Velcro into 2 pieces, each $2 1/2$" long. Separate hook sides from loop sides and sew to inside top of bag.

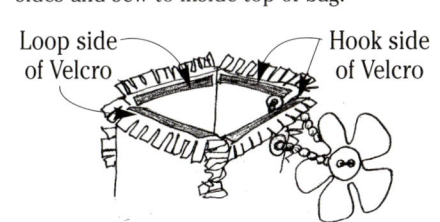

5. **Flower:** Place 2 different prints, right sides together, on the flower die and cut 1 flower with 2 different sides.
6. With right sides together, sew a $1/8$" seam around the flower leaving an opening for turning. Clip curves and turn right side out. Stuff and sew the opening closed.
7. Sew eyelets at ends of chain, one on each side of the flower center. Sew a button on each side of flower over eyelets. When open, the container can hold a hot or cold drink. When closed, it can also be used as a cosmetic bag or change purse.

Wearables on the GO! 27

Snuggly Scarves to Keep You Warm

Snuggly Scarves

From classy to cuddly, scarves are a wardrobe essential. The Accu-Quilt GO! makes assembly so fast, you'll have the entire set done before you know it.

Make one in your favorite team colors to wear to the game. Wear one in your school colors to Homecoming and don't forget to match your favorite outfit.

This is a great project to share with children and teens.

instructions on pages 19 - 20

Wearables on the GO! 29

Batik Jacket

Make a jacket for your every mood, every passion, every interest. The colors say it all. Feeling breezy? Try a sky palette. Happy? Collect a fabric rainbow.

Let this gorgeous batik sample ignite your imagination. Strip sewing makes it simple. The Accu-Quilt GO! makes the cutting quick.

instructions on page 21

'Leather' Yoke Purse

Design an upscale look for a thrift shop price. Creating this purse is not just easy on the budget. The finished purse has a quality that will win the admiration of all your friends. It's destined to be your favorite purse.

instructions on page 21

Fully Accessorized

*Step out in style!
If unique is what you seek, this jacket and purse ensemble is a one of a kind fashionably made by You!*

Wearables on the GO! 31

for Baby Boys and Little Girls

Bibs for Girls and for Boys

If you are looking for an attractive and practical baby shower gift, bibs are always needed. Using the AccuQuilt GO! you can turn an inexpensive bib into a special gift. Have fun accessorizing your bears! Create just one, or a complete set for a truly memorable present.

instructions on pages 22 - 23

Adorable Bears

From the introduction of the Teddy Bear in 1902 to Winnie the Pooh, Captain Kangaroo's Dancing Bear and the famous Yogi Bear of Jellystone Park, children and adults have been in love with bears and bear motifs.

We grew up with them as companions and protectors. We dragged them about the house, dressed them up, and gave them tea parties.

The tradition continues with this delightful collection of appliques that you and your children will cherish.

Sweater Bear Onesie

Cute and cuddly, this bear keeps snuggly warm and so will your little one wearing this delightful onesie.

instructions on page 23

32   Wearables on the GO!

Ballet Bear Pink Sweatshirt Dress

Decked out in lace tu-tus, these ballet bears stand ready to pirouette into position on your little girl's newest favorite frock.

instructions on page 23

Wearables on the GO! 33

Vivian Peritts

Vivian is an accomplished designer, author, inventor, artist, and fan of the AccuQuilt GO!.

Her multi-media signature style often incorporates repetitive shapes "but precision has always been a challenge."

"The GO! Cutting system makes everything 'GO' together beautifully." Vivian's creative expertise with crafts, sewing, and décor comes to the fore in this fabulous new collection of projects.

Always on the cutting edge, Vivian presents innovative ways to reuse, remix and bring new life to existing products. Fans will recognize Vivian from her appearances on national TV programs.

SUPPLIERS
Most quilt and fabric stores carry an excellent assortment of supplies. If you need something special, ask your local store to contact the following companies.

DIE-CUTTER and DIES FOR CUTTING with AccuQuilt® GO!™ Fabric Cutter and GO! Fabric Cutting Dies
  AccuQuilt - accuquilt.com
FABRICS
  Moda Fabrics - unitednotions.com
  Henry Glass & Co.
  Clothworks
  Studio e Fabrics
  Robert Kaufman
INTERFACING and STABILIZER:
  Bosal
  ThermOWeb
PIPING, HEM TAPE, BIAS TAPE:
  Wrights
FELT and BAMBOO FELT
  National Nonwovens
EMBROIDERY FLOSS and PEARL COTTON:
  DMC
HOOK and LOOP TAPE:
  Velcro
BUTTONS:
  Blumenthal Lansing
  Dritz
BEADS, JEWELRY FINDINGS, CHAINS:
  Blue Moon Beads
  La Petite
CRYSTAL BEADS:
  Swarovski

MANY THANKS to my staff for their cheerful help and wonderful ideas!
Kathy Mason • Patty Williams
Donna Kinsey • Kristy Krouse
David & Donna Thomason

Comfortable and cute, these dresses are perfect for playtime, party time or anytime.

Construction is quick and easy. Your little girl is going to want an entire wardrobe of these fabulous outfits.

Pillow Case Dress
Too cute! Ribbons tie at the shoulders for a designer touch. Tie a ribbon about the waist for a matching sash.
instructions on page 24

34 Wearables on the GO!